THE
GUIDE TO
PURCHASING
AN
ORIENTAL RUG

Jan David Winitz
&
The Breema Rug Study Society

Color Plates
Dennis Anderson Photo-Publishing

Published by:
The Breema Rug Study Society
Oakland, California USA

As the young children watch, tribal Turkoman women begin weaving a room-size carpet.

Rugs photographed are from the collections of
Manocher Movlai and Jan David Winitz.

Rug Restoration:
Breema Gallery Restoration Department,
Gretchen Brandt, Coordinator.

This book was conceived, designed, and produced
by The Breema Rug Study Society.

Technical Information: Gretchen Brandt

Co-published by
The Breema Rug Study Society &
Dennis Anderson Photo-Publishing

Library of Congress Catalog Card Number 84-071493
ISBN 0-930021-00-2

CONTENTS

PLATE 1

Introduction

Some years ago, I reluctantly accompanied a friend in the search for an antique rosewood table. Among countless other shops, our pursuit brought us to one small establishment, tucked back from a busy city street. As my friend became enthralled in a discussion of a Queen Anne double dome bureau, I wandered to a far corner of the store, where I noticed the edge of an oriental rug barely visible under a massive oak chest. The sight of the rug's clear colors and boldly-knotted patterns brought back memories of my grandmother's house, where as a child I was fascinated by the detailed designs of the carpets which covered her floors.

Intrigued, I requested that the proprietor move the chest in order that I might see the complete rug. Unearthed from its obscure location and placed in a sunny spot near the front window, the small piece glowed. Much to the surprise of both my friend and the shopkeeper, I purchased the rug immediately.

Once at home, I hung the rug in my study. After devoting some time to research, I found that I owned a Kazak carpet, made some 70 years before by tribespeople who inhabited the rugged Caucasus Mountains. My Kazak did not remain my only carpet for very long. Through the process of buying more rugs, I honed my taste and learned how to avoid potential pitfalls.

In the course of my research, I met several people who were also intrigued by the study of oriental carpets. Together we began an informal study group to share both the rugs and information we were lucky enough to acquire. We were particularly fortunate to meet Manocher Movlai, a Kurdish tribesman who grew up in an isolated rug-weaving village in the Near East, and later travelled extensively among the many carpet-making peoples. As a member of our newly-formed Breema Rug Study Society, Mr. Movlai was able to give us otherwise unobtainable information, as well as an original perspective on our western sources.

One evening, after the Society had given a workshop on purchasing oriental rugs, a participant asked for some suggestions for further reading. I mentioned a few appropriate texts, at which she replied that she didn't have the time to make an exhaustive study. What she was interested in was a concise, practical guide.

1. MALAYER (Persia)   early 20th century   4ft 8in x 6ft 8in

Oriental rugs are unique as works of art which also serve a functional purpose. Their bold, intricate designs and striking combinations of color are equally intriguing and mysterious. Becoming familiar with rugs in terms of design, color, quality of materials, level of craftsmanship, and decorative and investment value, is an invaluable asset in making the most appropriate purchase.

Having heard this from so many other newcomers to oriental rugs, my inspiration was kindled. That evening, I went home and began work on the first draft of what eventually grew into *The Guide To Purchasing An Oriental Rug.*

The result is a book which I believe is highly informative, to-the-point and readable. I have intentionally left the text brief enough that it can easily be absorbed in its entirety. I suggest that you read it once through, and then return to the most relevant sections for closer examination. When you are ready to go to a dealer to search for a rug, bring this handbook with you. Refer to its guidelines for finding the most suitable rug and show the dealer the plates of the pieces whose color, design and overall composition you find most appealing. Enjoy, as I did when I made my first purchase, the experience of discovering the rug which is both the most appropriate and inspiring.

By the way, that small Kazak is still hanging in my study. It has served as a fitting reminder that my aim has been to offer a practical handbook which will aid the reader in making a purchase which is both educated and enjoyable.

2. QASHQAI (Persia)   circa 1900   4ft 1in x 5ft 6in
A superb example of the spontaneous creativity of tribal weaving. Notice the myriad of woven animals, flowers, crosses and other figures characteristic of rugs from South Persia.

PLATE 2

PLATE 3

Types Of Oriental Rugs

The term "oriental rug" applies to hand-knotted carpets woven in the East over a wide area extending from the Balkans into China. As the weaving is not performed by machine, oriental rugs have a particular sense of aliveness and individuality which attests to the craftsmanship and artistry invested in their creation. The materials used are natural—primarily wool and cotton, with occasional goat hair, camel hair and silk.

As you begin to look at oriental rugs, it is useful to become familiar with a simple system of classifying the various types you will see. Basically, all oriental rugs can be grouped under two major headings: *traditional* rugs and *contemporary* rugs.

Traditional oriental rugs refer to those woven in Persia, the Caucasus, Central Asia, Afghanistan, Turkey and China. They are the result of a carpet-making heritage of at least 700 years. This category of rugs can be further divided into pieces of either "tribal", "city" or "town" origin.

The designation "tribal" pertains to rugs created in either a nomadic or village setting, using methods and designs traditional to the specific ethnic group to which the weaver belongs. Most tribal rugs are knotted by either an individual or an entire family employing designs which are usually geometric and abstract.

Working within the guidelines of their particular weaving heritage, the tribal rug-makers spontaneously create details of their own inspiration, as they build their carpets row-by-row. In tribal rugs, individuality is encouraged, as it is an expression of the weaver's own creativity. Often, the rug-maker will weave a particular repeated pattern throughout the field of the rug, only to alter it dramatically near the end of the piece. Tribal rugs contain numerous hidden mysteries. I lived with one South Persian Afshar rug for almost a year before I noticed a tiny woven gazelle grazing in one corner of the piece.

Many tribal weavers participate in every phase of the rug-making process. They are often the shepherds who shear the wool for their carpets from their own sheep, as well as the dyers who create a stunning array of colors from natural vegetal and mineral sources.

3. KASHAN (Persia)   early 20th century   4ft 4in x 6ft 5in
Woven in a traditional city rug-making center, this piece has a lush, finely-knotted floral design. The central medallion provides an overall balance and focus to the seemingly endless array of tendrils, blossoms and vines.

With the advent of modernization in the rug-weaving world, the making of carpets is quickly becoming a vanishing art among the tribal peoples. As a result, almost all old tribal rugs are increasing in value. Today, few tribal groups continue to weave high quality carpets using the old methods.

Traditional "city" rugs are made by groups of weavers in a workshop setting, predominantly in Persia and Turkey. They use primarily floral designs which are linked directly to the famous Persian Court Carpets of the 15th – 17th centuries, as well as to much earlier traditions. City rugs are typified by their tightness of weave and complex, carefully-planned patterns, in contrast to the more stylized and spontaneous designs of the tribal pieces.

In the workshop setting, the weavers are skilled craftsmen who follow a knot-by-knot blueprint provided them by a professional carpet designer. The weavers' task is to follow this pattern to absolute perfection. The designer, who is often a highly trained master artist, strives to create a rug which in its overall design and color combination will endlessly impress and fascinate the viewer.

Through a rich display of swirls, tendrils, rosettes and arabesques, the artist demonstrates the tremendous dexterity of his craft: the ability to compose a highly creative expression which follows the perfect order of the universe. The careful discipline of a fine artist can be seen in that even the smallest motif of his overall pattern is positioned with exactness to create a definite effect.

Within the seemingly constant movement of a superb city carpet, there exists an infinite depth of stillness and calm. This is the quality which unifies the carpet into a harmonious artistic statement. In short, excellence in city weaving is measured by the rug's overall sense of balance in its composition and the technical perfection in the execution of its design.

A third subcategory of traditional oriental carpets are those pieces which could be called "town" rugs. Usually woven in the small workshops of the larger villages in the vicinity of major trading centers, these provide the bridge between the nomadic or village tribal pieces and the city carpets. Town rugs usually employ primarily floral designs that have been reduced to the more rectilinear proportions of the geometric tribal pieces. The weavers often follow blueprints to create their designs and select their colors, but the element of spontaneity is also present. In short, town rugs offer the superb sense of movement and fascinating intricacy of the city carpets coupled with the bold directness of the tribal weavings.

In addition to those still being woven today throughout traditional rug-making areas, a significant number of *contemporary* rugs come from non-traditional weaving regions, such as India, Pakistan, Bulgaria and Romania. These differ from traditional rugs in that the designs that the weavers use are not part of their cultural heritage.

Many contemporary rugs are faithful reproductions of historically-important and striking motifs, while an increasing number reinterpret traditional designs and color combinations to

4. EZINE (Turkey)   contemporary
(left) 2ft 9in x 4ft 11in   (right) 2ft 5in x 4ft 5in
These contemporary pieces demonstrate the Turkish rug-makers' return to traditional village designs and to the use of the natural dyeing process. The blue is extracted from the indigo plant, the red from madder and the yellow from onion, camomile and other vegetal sources.

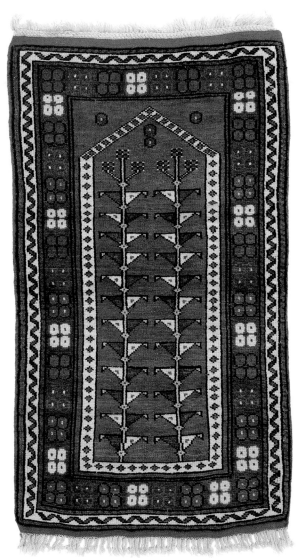

PLATE 4

PLATE 5

make them more compatible with modern decorating styles. The designs reproduced in contemporary rugs are almost unlimited. Patterns traditional to the cities of Kashan and Tabriz, the towns of Heriz, Ḳaraja and Meymeh, and the tribal Turkoman, Caucasian and Qashqai are among those incorporated into contemporary rugs.

The quality of contemporary rugs being produced in more recently developed weaving areas has increased dramatically. The finest workshops of regions such as India, Pakistan, the Balkans and Egypt are now employing a level of craftsmanship, quality of wool and clarity of design which rivals that of carpets currently made in traditional weaving regions.

Several types of rugs now being produced are distinctive in their simple beauty, popularity among home decorators and reasonable prices. A revival of the use of traditional village patterns and natural vegetal dyes is now being seen in Turkish rugs woven primarily in the small towns near Ezine and Bergama. These rugs are significant in their bold, clear patterns and their rich shades of blue (from indigo), yellow (from onion skins) and red (from the madder plant), along with undyed white wool.

The Gabbeh is a thick pile rug which uses the simple, irregular geometric patterns of the South Persian nomads. Woven diamonds, stars, crosses and animals adorn the field. Gabbehs, made at present predominantly in Romania, are unusual among oriental rugs in their exclusive use of earth tones, such as tan, beige, rust and sand.

A shepherd and his sheep return to their village at dusk.

5. GABBEH (Romania)   contemporary   4ft 7in x 6ft 2in
Reproducing the patterns and colors of the weavings of the South Persian nomads, the contemporary Gabbeh retains the powerful simplicity and balance of the tribal rug-making tradition. This Romanian carpet is characterized by high quality wool, a sturdy foundation and thick pile.

The Basics Of Structure

The creation of an oriental carpet is a lengthy process, yet to understand the structure of a carpet is not difficult. Once the basic framework is grasped, it will be easy for the potential buyer to take into account a number of rug facts that initially seem mysterious.

Oriental rugs are divided by weaving techniques into two categories—pile carpets and flatwoven carpets. A pile carpet has a velvety surface which is produced by adding loops of yarn around the foundation threads and then shearing them to the desired length. Flatweaves have a smooth knotless surface.

FOUNDATION. The foundation of an oriental rug consists of vertical warp threads and horizontal weft threads. The first step in the actual weaving process is to stretch the warp threads taut on a loom. The weft is then drawn over one warp thread and under the next, from one edge of the rug to the other, perpendicular to the warp. The weft threads are turned and woven back across the rug, creating a finished edge. The fringe is actually the ends of the warp threads. Close examination of the fringe will enable one to determine from what material the foundation of a particular rug is made. Wool and cotton are the fibers that are most often used for this purpose. Wool feels like hair and has a bristly appearance, while cotton is smoother to the touch and has a bright white color. Some finely-woven carpets use silk foundations.

PILE CARPETS. In this type of carpet, after the placement of several rows of weft, a complete horizontal row of knots is tied. Each knot is looped securely around a pair of warp threads and then clipped, giving the knot a distinct head and tail. The head secures the fluffy tail which creates the pile surface. Again several weft threads are woven across the warp. Every knot is now supported by a weft thread above and below it and by a warp thread on either side.

The knots are generally either of two major types, the symmetrical and the asymmetrical, also known as the Turkish or Ghiordes and the Persian or Senneh, respectively. The difference between the two knots is in the way they are looped around their pairs of warp threads. The asymmetrical knot allows for a more intricate design, as in traditional city weavings and tribal Turkoman carpets. Symmetrical knots, generally found in Caucasian and many Turkish rugs, lend themselves to bold designs.

It is fascinating to realize that unlike the painter, who is able to add color and tone to his composition as a whole to insure that the desired effect is achieved, the weaver constructs a carpet row-by-row. She cannot turn back. To retie a knot several inches away means unravelling several hours of work. Neither can she place a knot ahead as a marker for the future, as a knot can only be tied directly above the finished portion of the carpet. Every knot in an oriental carpet must be tied with individual care and a knowledge of its position in the design as a whole.

This knowledge should be helpful in viewing a pile carpet at close range. Not only will the viewer gain an appreciation of the many months, or in some cases years, spent in creating an oriental rug, but will also discover many surprising details, as in an oriental carpet each knot is unique.

FLATWEAVES. Several techniques are used to create the pileless flatweave carpets. The most common type of flatweave, the *kelim,* is almost identical in appearance on both front and back. Design is created not from the addition of knots, but from color changes in the horizontal weft threads. Kelims were traditionally made by many tribal peoples who often wove pile rugs as well.

Another flatweave technique, *soumak,* results from the addition of extra wefts which are not actually part of the foundation of the piece. While both the kelim and the soumak have a smooth face, the back of the soumak has many uncut dangling threads. Sometimes a piece is seen where pile and flatweave techniques are combined. This provides an interesting visual and textural contrast.

Pictured is a small section of a carpet viewed from both front and back. On the front surface the pile is visible as knot heads and bristly tails. On the underside of the carpet the structural components are visible.

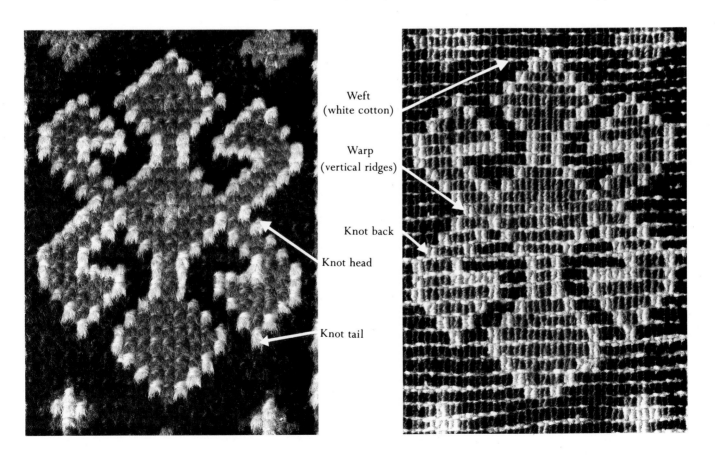

Weft
(white cotton)

Warp
(vertical ridges)

Knot back

Knot head

Knot tail

PLATE 6

Viewing An Oriental Rug

One chooses to furnish one's home with oriental rugs for several reasons. The carpets serve as durable, long-lasting floor coverings, adding comfort and warmth to the environment. Most importantly, they are handcrafted works of art, which provide unmatched beauty and grace. As with any art form, in order to truly appreciate oriental rugs, one must learn how to properly look at them. "Educated viewing" is a valuable aid in choosing the rug that is certain to provide years of enjoyment.

In looking at oriental rugs, always strive to view them in the light of appreciation rather than of criticism. Each rug is the product of highly-skilled craftsmen who developed their physical dexterity and sense of artistic balance over a number of years. An almost incomprehensible amount of creative effort goes into the making of each rug. A finely-woven room-size carpet may take a group of weavers over a year to complete. Some larger nomadic carpets are the result of three or more years of effort by a single rugmaker.

When looking at a rug, as when viewing a landscape, position yourself so that you can see the entire piece at a single glance. Notice what it is about the piece that catches your attention first. Do you relate easily to its overall design and combination of colors?

Be sure to view a rug from two or more vantage points. As the rug absorbs or reflects light differently from each new angle, you will be surprised to notice that the colors take on strikingly varied hues and the design a somewhat new appearance.

After getting a general impression of the rug, examine its design elements more closely. Most rugs are composed of a series of borders which serve to "frame" a central field. In the East, it is said that a rug's borders provide a window to the mysteries of the universe and that what we view in the field actually extends infinitely in each direction.

6. HERIZ (Persia)   circa 1900   8ft x 11ft 6in

This Northwest Persian carpet belongs to the "town" rug-making category, possessing both the tremendous activity of city pieces and the geometric lines of tribal weaving. In the midst of an intensity of movement is a delightful central flower. Notice that the weaver intentionally placed the innermost diamond of the flower off-center.

7. TURKOMAN TEKKE (Central Asia)   circa 1900   3ft 5in x 6ft 5in

Fine Turkoman rugs such as this use intricately-woven details which have an extraordinary sharpness and clarity. Notice that at both ends of the rug the border is replaced by a "skirt" of pine branches, a design element seen only in Turkoman weaving. Here, simple color creates a powerful effect, especially in the numerous shades of naturally-dyed red.

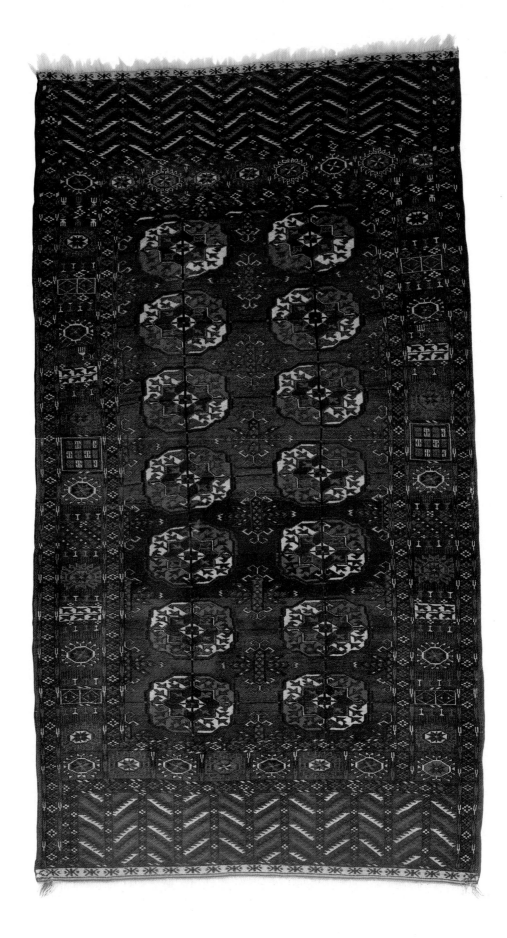

PLATE 7

PLATE 8

PLATE 9

Take note of the rug's main border and its narrower supporting or secondary borders. Each border may be totally distinctive in terms of design, yet the weaver's aim is to include certain elements which are common in all of them, lending a unified, balanced appearance.

Focus now on the field of the rug. Does it have the strong focal point of one or more predominant medallions or is it covered with a repetitive overall design?

The magic of the master weaver's art lies in the ability to create unity, in the rug as a whole as well as in the relationship between individual details. Step forward to focus on the individual patterns. Perhaps you see a tiny animal, the delicately drawn details in a series of flowers or triangular forms resembling mountains. Look at each detail in relation to the larger pattern of which it is a part. Examine how the larger design complements both the section of the rug to which it belongs and the piece as a whole. You can see that even a tiny cross in one corner of the field is harmonious in terms of shape, size and location with the entire rug.

As well as being a visual delight, getting to know an oriental rug is a tactile experience. Be sure to touch the rug and experience the quality of the wool. Wool can differ dramatically in terms of durability and resiliency depending upon the conditions under which the sheep were raised and from what part of the animal it was taken.

One of the highest quality fibers is "mountain oily wool", shorn from sheep raised at high elevations in regions of Persia such as Kurdistan and the Zagros range. Mountain sheep are vital and healthy, as they graze the rocky slopes in cool mountain temperatures. Their wool is renowned for its strength and high lanolin content.

Finally, view at least one corner of the rug from the back. Look closely at the structure of the rug, consisting of rows of tiny knots woven onto a framework of vertical and horizontal foundation threads. Notice that the design of a hand-made pile rug shows on the back as well as on the front. This is the definitive way of verifying that a rug is hand-made, as machine-manufactured rugs show the design little or not at all from the back. Rug experts can tell a tremendous amount from examining the back of a carpet. Information such as size of knots, color of the horizontal weft threads, and whether the surface is flat or ridged can be clues to the exact region in which a rug was made.

Look at oriental rugs as genuine works of art, which as you become familiar with them, will reveal endless surprises and delight. Overall, you will find that the closer you look at a fine carpet, the more your mind will become interested and your feelings inspired.

8. KURDISH RUNNER (Persia)   late 19th century   4ft 2in x 11ft

Many traditional Kurdish rugs use fields of delightful spring flowers (here derived from the "boteh" or paisley design) and an abundance of naturally dyed colors; in this case, red, blue, green, yellow, black and pink. Notice that the floral motif is echoed in the diagonally striped borders.

9. KAZAK (Caucasus)   late 19th century   2ft 8in x 3ft 6in

This highly original piece has a distinctive, playful quality. It vividly demonstrates how the border is a frame which acts as a window to the universe, represented by the field. Notice that the background blue color changes suddenly near the bottom of the field, a mark of individuality in tribal weaving.

PLATE 10

22

Determining The Type Of Rug
You Wish to Own

When you attempt to choose a single carpet from the wide variety on the market, your selection can be a difficult one. In reaching a decision concerning which rug to buy, most potential buyers have two major considerations: practicality and aesthetics. Asking yourself the following four questions can be an effective start toward choosing the carpet that is right for you.

An important initial question might be—where in my home or office am I planning to put an oriental rug? Perhaps you are seeking a carpet that will be the central focus of your living room. As a preliminary step, be sure to take accurate measurements of the area. Let's say the room is 12' x 16'. In this case, you might feel that a 9' x 12' rug would be appropriate. Not necessarily so. A particular carpet may appear substantially larger or smaller than its actual dimensions depending on its design and use of color.

For instance, floral carpets with designs which repeat throughout the field tend to blend with their surroundings. On the other hand, geometric rugs with their predominant medallions and abstract designs command more attention. Accordingly, a space for which a 9' x 12' floral carpet is appropriate could be accommodated by a geometric rug 8' x 10' or smaller. This, of course, can only be used as a general guideline. It is best to set flexible maximum and minimum size limits to compensate for the various effects that different rugs will have in your room.

Your second question might be—is the spot where I would like to place the rug a light, medium or heavy traffic area? Depending upon their condition and age, various rugs will have different uses. For instance, a stunning, semi-antique carpet might quickly be ruined in a central passageway, yet would offer many years of beauty if located in a quiet niche or less busy room. An antique prayer rug which is low in pile yet still vivid in design may not be suitable for the floor at all, but could become the striking centerpiece of an entire room if hung on the wall.

Be especially careful in considering a rug that is to be placed under the dining room table. Because it must withstand the effects of chairs being moved across it, the rug chosen for a dining room used on a daily basis should be in particularly good condition.

Your next question might be the most practical of all—what is my price range? It is important to set both your ideal price and your upper limit early on in your search. As you begin to look at rugs, you will soon discover if the price you have decided on is realistic in terms of the type of carpet you wish to own. If it isn't, it may be helpful to consider in which areas you are

10. QASHQAI (Persia)   circa 1900   4ft 1in x 5ft 6in
Geometric design rugs with repeated medallions command attention. Here, the restrained use of white offset by deep indigo blue is used to outline and highlight the major design elements. Rugs with a rich array of detail can hold the interest of their owners for years.

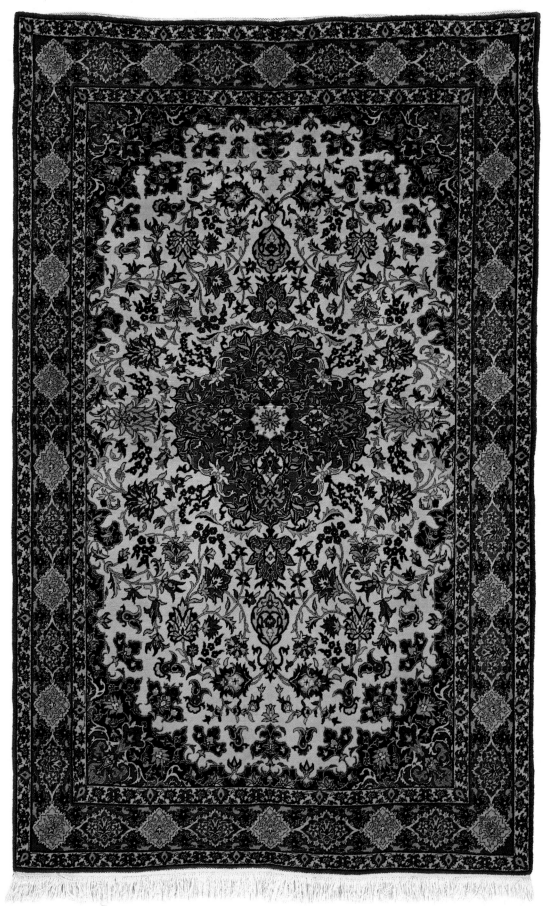

PLATE 11

willing to compromise in order to find a piece that is within your price range. Size, type, age and condition are some of the factors which can determine the cost of a rug. Price may also be substantially affected by the current demand for a particular rug, its availability and the rarity of its design.

In any case, there are many beautiful rugs on the market at all price levels from a few hundred to many thousands of dollars. As a general rule, it is more advisable to buy a carpet that is within your price range than to wait and save for a more expensive piece. Most authentic hand-made oriental rugs have a remarkably high resale value. When you are financially able to make the larger purchase, you will most likely be able to exchange your rug for at least the same price for which you bought it. Meanwhile, having the rug in your home will help to increase your knowledge of your own taste in the enchanting world of oriental rugs.

Your final consideration is of equal importance to the preceding three—what are my aesthetic preferences and what type of carpet will satisfy them? Surprisingly, decor is not as much of a deciding factor as one might think, as their stylization and age-old designs make most oriental rugs compatible with almost any room setting. Use your decorating considerations, such as matching the overall color scheme of your room, as guidelines rather than limitations. I have all too often seen customers decide against the rug they really loved because of unrealistic decorating constraints. A hand-made rug is not a standard item, so refrain from having standard expectations about it. For the most part, you can rarely go wrong if the rug you choose is the one that you relate to the most. Further discussion of how to integrate a rug into your room can be found in the chapter on decorating.

Especially if you are a newcomer to oriental rugs, it is recommended that you look closely at the color plates contained in this book, as they represent fine examples of the many rug-weaving traditions. In doing so, you may find that you relate most to the simple geometric patterns and bold display of color found in traditional Caucasian and contemporary Turkish rugs (see plates 9 & 4). Or perhaps you'll favor the intricately-detailed, more deeply-colored work of the Qashqai tribespeople (plate 2). Maybe it is a contemporary Balkan or Indian carpet with a lush floral design that will most suit your taste (plate 11).

So, supported by your notes concerning location, possible sizes, price range and a particular weaving tradition or design which you are attracted to, you are ready to visit a rug store. It is always preferable to deal with established galleries that you have heard about through someone whose opinion you respect. Reputable dealers will back up their rugs over time through reasonable exchange policies, as their business depends upon being responsive to the needs of their customers.

In the store, refer often to the notes you've made, as they speak for both your practical and aesthetic motivations for buying an oriental rug. This will give you a sense of clarity and direction in the face of the many rugs you will see.

11. BALKAN ISFAHAN (Romania)   contemporary   5ft 10in x 10ft 5in
This is an example of the high quality contemporary rugs being produced in non-traditional weaving areas. This piece, reproducing the traditional design of the Persian city weaving center of Isfahan, is richly-detailed, with an exceptional ruby-colored medallion highlighted by an ivory field.

PLATE 12

At the Rugstore

YOUR FIRST LOOK

In the store, let your own sense of balance and beauty be your guide. Refrain from choosing a rug that you don't have a particular affinity toward simply because it is in vogue or seems to be an irresistible bargain. Acquiring a carpet under these circumstances often leads to disappointment later on. Remember, the rug you purchase may be a companion for a number of years.

Have the dealer show you an assortment of pieces that fit the description you've created in your notes. Be on the lookout for the following indications that you've found a rug which you are compatible with.

Is there one rug to which you experience an instant attraction? Look at several more rugs and then come back to this one. Do you have a similar favorable reaction on second viewing? Oftentimes, this spontaneous admiration is as much a key to one's real taste as is close inspection and careful deliberation.

If no one rug you have seen immediately seems to jump out and speak to you, which piece remains most in your mind? Perhaps there is one Persian Kashan which has a vivid floral design that you can still visualize clearly or a Central Asian Turkoman with a shade of red that you found particularly attractive. Ask to see this rug again—perhaps it is the one.

One means of finding a suitable rug is to search for those pieces whose combination of colors you find most appealing. In the rug-making countries of the East, buyers often choose rugs primarily by color. They know that color is the key to design, accentuating particular patterns and subduing others. The colors in a rug that you're considering should be in balance with one another and pleasing to your own artistic sense.

Unless they discover a rug which they are certain suits both their aesthetic taste and practical needs, I always recommend to my customers that they see one or more pieces in their own home before coming to a final decision. From my experience, a reputable dealer will be more than happy to either bring the rugs into your home himself or allow you to take them out on approval.

At home, place the rug or rugs in the area you've chosen. Give each rug ample opportunity to reveal its true attributes before making a final judgment about it. Rearrange the furniture

12. KURDISH (Persia)   circa 1900   4ft 5in x 6ft 5in

In the Orient, many rug buyers select carpets primarily by their use of color. This piece employs the artist's entire pallet of color, yet through skillful dyeing, placement and use of proportion, the great variety of hues fits together into a harmonious whole. Notice that the field of this carpet has no clearly defined background or foreground.

slightly; try the rug in a different direction or a new spot; be adventurous. This way, you will be able to more accurately determine the possibilities for each rug you are considering, how it fits in your room and if it is complementary to your furniture and overall decor. Occasionally, a rug which you were attracted to in the store will not have the same appeal in the home environment. Then again, I've often seen a new rug settle into a spot so perfectly that it seemed to have been there for years! In short, seeing a rug in the actual home environment for a short period of time is often the surest way to find out whether or not it suits your taste and needs.

A CLOSER EXAMINATION

Before coming to a final decision to buy a certain rug, it is important to examine it from a somewhat more critical standpoint. Watch out for a few major problems which, if they show up in a rug, should probably dissuade you from selecting it. Look at the back of the rug. If the foundation is broken at any point or there is evidence of moth damage, seen most commonly by the undersides of the knots being eaten away, the piece is less than structurally sound. Mildew damage, called dry rot, manifests as brittleness and cracking at the foundation. The rug may also have a dank, musty odor. Check to see that a rug which you intend to put on the floor sits flat. If it doesn't, the elevated areas will tend to wear at a disproportionately quick rate.

Along with the potentially major problems listed above, there are also a few apparent "flaws" which can actually work to the advantage of the customer. They are usually minor and at the same time can substantially reduce the dealer's asking price. For instance, it is not unusual for a rug to be wider at one end than at the other. A difference in width of 1-4 inches measured across the top and bottom of a medium-sized rug is considered acceptable, as it is characteristic of the handweaving process. A more perceptible width difference of 4-6 inches can normally be stretched back into shape by a competent restoration specialist.

If the cords binding the edges of the rug are frayed or missing or the ends are just beginning to unravel, know that this can also be rectified inexpensively.

Don't dismiss a rug because it is dirty. Often after cleaning, the color will improve substantially. If a rug you have an interest in is noticeably dirty, consider putting a deposit down on the piece and asking the dealer to have it washed before you come to your final decision about it.

Although it is important to search out any substantial problems a rug may have, it is advisable to be tolerant of a few minor signs of normal wear. This is especially true when looking at older rugs. As I couldn't refrain from saying to a customer who commented negatively on a small low pile area in an antique Caucasian prayer rug: "I only hope that both of us could be in such good condition when we're 100 years old."

DISPELLING COMMON RUG MYTHS

Many of my customers have found that some of the seemingly logical information they have about oriental rugs is actually misconception. One common misnomer is that a heavy, thick rug is

13. QASHQAI KELIM (Persia)   circa 1900   5ft 8in x 8ft 9in
When considering what type of oriental rug to purchase, don't overlook the flatweave. Kelims (or flatweaves which are almost identical in appearance on both front and back) are distinctive in their clear colors, bold designs and exceptional durability.

PLATE 13

PLATE 14

always superior to a thinner one. A heavier feel in a rug results from thicker threads used in the foundation and a higher cut pile. Neither of these techniques are intended to increase durability. In fact, a rug with a less firm handle or low cut pile can be just as durable. In addition, the closely cut pile allows for an intricacy of design which is impossible to achieve when the nap is left long. High pile is commonly found in contemporary Indian and Tibetan rugs, as well as in those of the tribal weavers living in cold, mountainous areas, such as parts of Northwest Persia and the Caucasus.

Soft wool is not necessarily better wool. High quality wool has three vital characteristics: sheen, strength and elasticity. It contains a natural lanolin content which you can feel. In contrast, soft, fluffy wool may lack the needed durability. Be sure to avoid buying a rug in which the wool is coarse and dry. This can be the result of over-processing or heavy chemical washing.

Often, newcomers to oriental rugs are concerned that the design of the rug they choose is exactly symmetrical and the borders perfectly rectangular. This can be an important factor in judging the quality of traditional city rugs and of contemporary rugs reproducing city designs. However, in tribal and town rugs the fact that a medallion may be slightly askew, a figure irregularly drawn, is hardly seen as distracting. In fact, irregularity is one of the lures of tribal weaving, as it marks the rug-maker's individuality and spontaneous creativity.

Some rug buyers mistakenly avoid carpets with synthetic dyes, fearing that they are harsh, will run easily and be damaging to the wool. While this was true of the aniline dyes brought to the rug-making world in the mid-19th century and then banned in Persia during one period in the early-1900's, modern chrome-based dyes are reliable, colorfast and available in an array of tasteful colors. Especially when considering rugs woven in the mid-20th century or later, make your choice based on whether the colors are pleasing and in harmony with one another rather than on the type of dyestuffs which were used. It is primarily those who are purchasing older carpets for collection purposes who insist on pieces which use predominantly dyes obtained from natural sources.

The most common myth of all is that a tightly woven rug is always more desirable than a more loosely woven one. In actuality, quality rugs can vary in knot count from 40 to over 600 knots per square inch. For instance, 100 knots per square inch is considered to be fine for a Caucasian Kazak, yet very coarse for a Persian Kerman. The loosely woven Kazak may be of equal or greater value than a Kerman with triple the knot count.

In city-produced rugs, in which the weavers strive for exactness of detail, tightness of weave can be one factor which determines craftsmanship. In tribal pieces, knot count may be more a factor of technique than of quality. For example, the sharply drawn medallions of Turkoman rugs necessitate a tight weave, while the large, bold designs of the various Turkish and Caucasian tribal groups are often executed more effectively with coarse knots than with fine ones.

14. BAKHTIARI-CHAHAR MAHAL (Persia)   circa 1940   4ft 7in x 6ft 8in
Members of the South Persian Bakhtiari tribe who have settled in the villages of the Chahar Mahal district weave highly decorative floral design carpets which retain the boldness and vigor of nomadic weaving. Bakhtiari rugs often have a remarkably high quality of wool which enhances durability and allows the dyes to penetrate more deeply into the fiber. This results in a clearer design and a richer color.

PLATE 15

Decorating Ideas

More and more, I find that my clients are furnishing their homes with oriental rugs without professional assistance, and that they, along with their family members, other relatives and friends, are approaching me for informal guidance. The ideas I offer them stem from my own experience of countless visits into my customers' homes to bring rugs on approval. As a result, I can definitively state that almost any high quality oriental rug can be integrated into the home environment. All that is needed is creativity and a few practical guidelines.

Through repeated experience, I have found that the most useful guide in finding the appropriate rug for your home is a simple one—to discover what your own taste in carpets is and to seek out rugs which suit it. Whether intentionally or not, most people furnish their homes with items which are naturally complementary, that are compatible in style and tone. Yet, when the time comes to select an oriental rug, perhaps their most substantial purchase of all, they are hesitant to trust their natural preferences.

I'd like to give one concrete example to demonstrate this. Recently, an established client came to me to find a rug to be the central focus of her living room arrangement. She felt that because of the other furnishings and the predominant color scheme in the room, a Persian floral design carpet in shades of blue would be the most appropriate. In the store, she fell in love with a semi-antique Heriz carpet, which she was quick to disregard because of its geometric medallion and overall red coloring. After considerable discussion, I persuaded her to try it on approval.

In her home, she immediately protested, saying that the design was too large, and the shade of blue in the border too dark. She was right. According to conventional decorating standards, the rug just didn't work. I told her: "Wonderful. Having this rug in your home is teaching you what you need to know. Keep it for three days and learn all that you can." She agreed to do so, reluctantly.

On the second day, she called—to purchase the rug! That morning, when walking into the living room without thinking of the Heriz at all, she glanced at it and realized how wonderfully it fit into the room. Her experience was identical to that of many others. The unity that was created between the carpet she really loved and her other furnishings was greater than that which she could ever have achieved through calculated planning.

15. HERIZ (Persia)   early 20th century   9ft 6in x 14ft 11in
Fine rugs from the Northwest Persian weaving center of Heriz are impressive in appearance, yet comfortable to live with. Because of their predominant, spacious designs and warm, inviting use of color, they naturally become the focal point of any room.

In short, be open to a rug that you are attracted to, but which at first glance doesn't seem to conform to your decorating requirements. This is more advisable than purchasing a carpet which you are only marginally interested in, yet appears to fit in more easily with your other furnishings. And don't worry, for there are many simple, creative ways to assimilate your newly-purchased carpet into your overall decor. Below I have listed a few that I've found to be most effective.

First, roll up your sleeves and start to experiment with different placements of your furniture. Often, all that is necessary is to change the angle of a sofa or to move one chair to a new location. Only occasionally is a more extensive rearrangement needed. Second, consider adding other woven pieces, such as a bagface on the piano bench, a few antique rug pillows on the couch, or a decorative weaving on the wall. These small touches can bring a sense of balance and comfort to the room.

Other means of integrating a rug are a bit more ambitious. Bring accessories into your room which match a secondary color in your carpet. Perhaps echo the lines or patterns of the rug through the shapes of chairbacks or legs, window panes, vases or lamps. Be adventurous; experiment. Then, settle on one arrangement and sit with it for a day or two. This is the surest way to know if it creates the overall harmony which you desire.

Perhaps rather than introducing a rug into an established decorating scheme, you are starting with an empty room. In this case, you are in a particularly fortunate position. In fact, oftentimes in Europe, a newly-wed couple will receive an oriental rug as a gift from the bride's parents, who understand that a carpet is an effective starting point around which to base an entire decor.

To my clients who are starting from "scratch", I usually recommend that they begin slowly. Don't rush. Purchase a single rug and live with it for awhile. Then add another carpet that complements your room and nourishes your aesthetic sensibilities. Remember that the great variety of colors and shades present in most oriental rugs will give you considerable flexibility in terms of the hues you decide to accent through the other furnishings in the room. Overall, this approach will enable your interior decorating to become an intriguing project rather than a burdensome chore.

Decorating your home with oriental rugs can be an exciting and fulfilling endeavor. It is an opportunity to create an environment that is satisfying, functional and distinctive. However, once you've settled on a pleasing arrangement, don't feel locked into it. Decorating is a joyful activity which is never really finished; there is always another creative touch to add. It is these lively additions which will keep your decor fresh and interesting.

16. KURDISH (Persia)   circa 1900   7ft 11in x 11ft
This Northern Persian carpet is an excellent example of the use of a repetitive "all-over" pattern, in this case the traditional "Mina Khani" design. This type of rug is more subtle in composition than those using predominant central medallions. Because of this, it serves to complement and accent the other furnishings in your room.

PLATE 16

How To Care For Your Rug

Oriental rugs are made to be lived on. In the East, nomads lay them out as protection against the desert floor, camels walk on them, and the Turkoman even use them as doors to their yurts, domed tent-like dwellings. The carpet you purchase may very well be the most durable furnishing in your home. If properly cared for, a high quality new carpet has an estimated floor life of at least seventy years.

The key to long carpet life is proper home care. The most important aspect is simply keeping your rug clean. It is recommended that a rug used on the floor be washed every three to five years. Wall rugs should be cleaned every five to eight years. It is advisable not to wait until the rug is visibly dirty, as dirt particles penetrate to the root of the pile, causing it to weaken and break. Oriental rugs should always be professionally hand-washed, never washed chemically or dry-cleaned. Only hand-cleaning by a competent specialist in oriental rugs protects against color run and assures revitalization of the wool. When selecting a cleaning service, be sure to ask directly if they have experience working with hand-made oriental rugs.

The second aspect of proper cleaning is to vacuum your rug regularly. Most oriental rugs can be safely vacuumed either on a weekly basis or when necessary. Smaller pieces should be turned over and their backs vacuumed monthly, while this should be done to larger pieces every six months. Obviously, older, fragile carpets cannot withstand frequent vacuuming. In this case, it is advisable to sweep your rug with either a broom or a manual carpet sweeper in the direction of the pile. This is easily determined by running your fingers across the carpet surface toward each fringe end and experiencing in which direction the pile lies down under your hand.

A carpet that is in use rarely suffers from moth damage if areas hidden under furniture are thoroughly vacuumed on a frequent basis. Casters should always be placed under furniture legs that rest on rug surfaces, as this minimizes the chance of crushed pile. Oriental rugs need special consideration to be safely stored. It is best to solicit the advice of an experienced restoration specialist.

To insure that your carpet continues to bring you joy for a long floor life, be sure to turn it regularly. Rugs positioned in areas of your home with established patterns of foot traffic should be switched in the opposite direction every six months to one year. Doing so virtually assures even wear of the rug surface.

Oriental rugs are made to be lived on, and an occasional spill is almost inevitable. As a general rule, immediately blot up as much of the moisture as possible with a clean towel, starting at the outer edge of the spill and working toward the center. Avoid rubbing, for it will only spread the stain further into the wool. Solid spills are best removed by carefully scooping them up with a spoon.

If your rug has been damaged by either wear or misuse, it is best to have it repaired before a more serious problem develops. A carpet generally shows wear first at the ends and edges. A process known as ''end-stopping'' prevents the rows of knots at the fringe ends from coming loose and falling out. This is accomplished by securing the outermost weft thread with a blanket stitch visible only from the back of the rug. Worn and unravelling edges can be rejuvenated by overcasting them with matching wool yarn, a technique called ''edge-binding''. If this is done as soon as wear begins to show, the underlying cords will not be damaged.

End-stopping and edge-binding are normal maintenance measures and most floor carpets must be cared for in this way two or more times during their life. Like other minor repairs, such as reknotting a small worn area or reweaving a tiny hole, they are surprisingly inexpensive.

Almost any damage to a carpet can be repaired, even larger holes. For more major repairs, it is wise to get one or more estimates from recommended restoration specialists. It is quite acceptable to insure competency by asking to see samples of their work. Remember that rug restoration is a highly developed skill and choosing a service simply because they offer the lowest estimate is not always advisable.

In deciding if you should have your rug repaired, ask what the value of the rug is in its present condition and what it will be when repaired. For restoration to be worthwhile in a practical sense, the value of the repaired rug should be greater than its value in the unrepaired state plus the cost of restoration. Extensive repairwork is becoming increasingly worthwhile on older pieces as they continue to grow more valuable and difficult to replace.

PLATE 17

Collecting Oriental Rugs

For centuries, Western man has been intrigued by oriental rugs. The very wealthy of Europe and, beginning in the late-1800's, the elite of the United States, have gone to great effort and expense to collect the finest examples of antique carpets. Today, high quality old rugs remain a central focus in the world of art investment.

Why collect oriental rugs? Works of art with true aesthetic grace and beauty have an appeal which is both universal and timeless. And as works of art, oriental rugs are products of human creativity and physical dexterity in their most developed form. In addition, oriental rugs are investments you can live on. They are unparalleled in their ability to add richness and grace to the home environment.

For at least a millennium, rug-weaving has been the predominant form of artistic and cultural expression among the numerous tribes of the Near East. Traditionally using all natural materials taken mostly from the local environment, the weaver labored between nine months to three years to create a functional art object which she may have intended to live with for the remainder of her life. Few art forms can rival oriental rugs in terms of the quality and quantity of human creative energy invested in them. As rugs made using the age-old methods and materials become increasingly rare, each fine old piece becomes a one-of-a-kind treasure.

Although investing in oriental rugs can be used as a short-term method of raising capital for only the very experienced, carpets have proven to be solid long-term investments. The investment value of a rug is determined by a number of factors, some extremely concrete, others equally intangible. As a guideline, consider as potentially collectible, rugs of antique (over 100 years old) and semi-antique (50 – 100 years old) vintage. For the most part, contemporary rugs should not be considered as collectible. Rather they should be purchased chiefly as beautiful, long-lasting home furnishings which retain their value over time.

The rug types which are most likely to have substantial collectible value are those woven by peoples whose art and culture have been thoroughly researched and documented. For example,

17. SHIRVAN & DAGHESTAN PRAYER RUGS (Caucasus)   late 19th century
(left) 2ft 8in x 6ft 1in   (right) 2ft 6in x 6ft 2in

Rugs originally intended to be used for prayer purposes are directional, with an arch-shaped niche, or "mihrab", in the upper portion of the field. Caucasian prayer rugs portray the bold, dignified character of the mountain weavers. Notice the rug-maker's comb woven in the prayer niche of each rug, possibly signifying the tribal belief in the sacredness of daily activity.

PLATE 18

Caucasian rugs, generally regarded as among the most collectible carpets on today's market, were appreciated only by a few serious collectors before a series of major exhibitions and books explored them beginning in the late-1960's. The same is true of village Anatolian (the high plains region located in modern day Turkey) and of Central Asian Turkoman carpets.

Keeping this in mind, the new collector might be wise to investigate the many fine examples made by weaving groups just beginning to be discovered by the mainstream of investors. Central in this category are the old rugs of the Kurdish tribespeople of northwestern Iran, Turkey and Iraq, and of the Baluche, located in the region along the Iran/Afghanistan border.

Historical significance is another tangible factor in determining collectible value. Rugs produced by weaving groups no longer in existence are prized as the surviving examples of artistic traditions which are lost forever. These include the weavings of the above-mentioned Caucasian tribespeople and the Salor and other tribes of the Turkoman. As always, it is the pieces which demonstrate the highest level of craftsmanship and artistry that should be viewed as the wisest investments.

Other rugs can be considered collectible based on attributes which are much more intangible. The most mature collectors seek out pieces which are exceptionally rare in design and color combination, and unsurpassed in craftsmanship. These are carpets with a power of creative expression that is literally unforgettable.

The new collector who is attempting to assess the artistic value of a rug should realize that it is a weaving with the strongest sense of overall harmony and a superb clarity of design which is most likely to pay lasting dividends. It is a common experience among collectors who have viewed two rugs made in the same village, of the same vintage and using similar designs, that one piece may reveal a much higher level of artistic achievement, originality and overall character. It may contain slight variations in color and pattern which make it truly exceptional. Remarkably, both rugs will often be in the same price range.

In fact, many of the most collectible pieces in terms of aesthetic value can be purchased at reasonable prices. This is because their hidden depth of artistic expression often goes unseen by many viewers. It is when the investor discovers this unexplored magical quality formerly hidden in a rug that the activity of collecting is most fulfilling.

18. BALUCHE BAGFACE (Persia)   circa 1900   1ft 7in x 2ft 5in

This stunning little bagface from the area in Eastern Persia near Torbat-i-Haidari, attests to the weaver's ability to create a striking effect with a limited pallet of colors. Characteristic of older Baluche weaving, the naturally-dyed colors employed are deep indigo blue, madder red and walnut brown, set off against a field of golden camel hair. The pattern is the "Tree of Life", a beloved Baluche motif.

19. TURKOMAN YOMUT (Central Asia)   circa 1880   6ft 10in x 9ft 6in

This Turkoman possesses all the attributes of a highly-collectible antique carpet. It is unsurpassed in its craftsmanship and artistry, which is clearly seen in its sharply delineated diagonal rows of Kepse Guls (Yomut central medallions). The use of color is extraordinary with varying shades of blue obtained from the roots, leaves and bark of the indigo plant, and "Turkoman Rust" from a dye-bath of madder root and cochineal. As well, the carpet is preserved in excellent condition.

20. KAZAK (Caucasus)   circa 1900   4ft 2in x 7ft 1in

Virtually neglected until the late-1960's, Caucasian rugs are now highly desirable to many serious collectors. This rug from the Kazak region is an example of the originality and power of Caucasian weaving. The bold geometric design and primary colors recall its rugged mountain origins.

PLATE 19

PLATE 20

PLATE 21

In the practical sense, when choosing rugs for investment purposes, collectors seek mostly those that contain vegetal and mineral dyes, as pieces colored with natural materials grow deeper and more vibrant in hue with age. Natural dyeing has been recognized as an art in itself and in the town or city setting, a master dyer might produce only a single color using a traditional family recipe. During this century, synthetic dyestuffs have been used extensively, giving any well-preserved old rug with naturally-dyed wool some collectible value.

The most established collectors seek out primarily exquisite pieces in exceptional condition. At this point, such rugs are in great demand, and, unfortunately, in short supply. For this reason, the new collector should not be discouraged from considering weavings with a few centimeters of knots missing, most likely at the fringe ends. A chief requirement should always be that the design is still vivid and the colors still true. Since the most established collectors overlook this type of rug, there are still many pieces on the market which demonstrate the optimum level of artistry and craftsmanship of the oriental rug-maker.

Investment in oriental rugs can be profitable and immensely gratifying. Yet, you must pay your dues. Extensive reading of the available literature on rug types, weaving techniques and the culture of the rug-making peoples is highly recommended, along with soliciting the counsel of more experienced collectors.

But the most essential qualification of all is to view as many rugs as possible, always maintaining an interest and openness to learn from the original artistic message that each fine weaving has to convey. For rugs do "speak" through their age-old designs, natural materials and the joyful energy invested in their creation. And it is only those collectors who develop ears to listen and eyes to see who will enter into a lifelong friendship with these products of the deepest creative impulse of man. Those who understand oriental rugs will agree that this is the most profitable investment of all.

21. BAKHTIARI CHAHAR-MAHAL (Persia)   late 19th century   5ft x 6ft 9in

In this piece is an expression of the joy that the oriental rug-maker experiences through her craft. Each panel tells its own story and could be considered a complete carpet in itself. Seemingly endless variation, masterful use of a wide range of naturally-obtained colors, and an overall sense of balance among diverse design elements give these carpets a power which for the collector is literally unforgettable.

22. TURKOMAN YOMUT ASMALYK (Central Asia)   circa 1880   3ft 11in x 1ft 6in
and CHUVAL   circa 1900   2ft 7in x 3ft 9in

The level of craftsmanship and artistry attained in the bags and decorative weaving of the nomadic Turkoman equals that found in their carpets. For this reason, many collectors specialize in smaller Turkoman pieces, such as the asmalyk, a trapping woven by a bride-to-be to decorate the flanks of her wedding camel. The chuval is the largest, and perhaps the most impressive, of the Turkoman storage bags.

PLATE 22

TECHNICAL
INFORMATION

Terms:

Warp: The vertical threads which run the length of the loom.

Weft: The horizontal threads which extend from one edge of the carpet to the other. They run perpendicular to, and are woven through the warp threads. Rows of pile knots are separated by one or more weft threads.

Shot: One pass of a weft thread from edge to edge of a rug.

Symmetrical knot: Also known as the Turkish or Ghiordes knot. The knot is tied on two warps and has a distinct head and tail. The tail lies directly under the head.

Asymmetrical knot: Also known as the Persian or Senneh knot. The knot head is looped around one warp thread. The tail is found beside the head, open to the left or right.

Z-spin & S-spin: When a material is spun into thread, the spindle is turned either clockwise which produces an "S" twist or counter-clockwise which creates a "Z" twist. Two or more of these threads are usually plied together for additional strength. Yarns that have been spun clockwise (S-spin) must be plied in a counter-clockwise direction (Z-spin) and vice versa. The notation z2s translates as two strands which have been spun counter-clockwise and then plied together in a clockwise direction.

1. Malayer 4′8″ x 6′8″
Warp: z5 cotton
Weft: Cotton, 1 shot
Knot: Symmetrical

2. Qashqai 4′1″ x 5′6″
Warp: z2s brown & cream wool
Weft: Tan wool, 2 shots
Knot: Asymmetrical to the left

3. Kashan 4′4″ x 6′5″
Warp: z4 cotton
Weft: Light blue cotton, 2 shots
Knot: Asymmetrical to the left

4. Turkish
On left 2′9″ x 4′11″
Warp: z2s cream wool
Weft: Cream wool, 2 shots
Knot: Symmetrical

On right 2′5″ x 4′5″
Warp: z2s cream wool
Weft: Cream wool, 2 shots
Knot: Symmetrical

5. Romanian Gabbeh 4′7″ x 6′2″
Warp: z2s ivory wool
Weft: Tan wool, 2 shots
Knot: Symmetrical

6. Heriz 8′ x 11′6″
Warp: z9 cotton
Weft: Cotton, 2 shots
Knot: Symmetrical

7. Turkoman 3′5″ x 6′5″
Warp: z2s ivory wool
Weft: Light grey wool, 2 shots
Knot: Asymmetrical to the right

8. Kurdish 4′2″ x 11′
Warp: z2s ivory wool
Weft: Rose wool, 1 shot
Knot: Symmetrical

9. Caucasian 2′8″ x 3′6″
Warp: z2s ivory, light grey & dark grey wool
Weft: Tan wool, 2 shots
Knot: Symmetrical

10. Qashqai 4′1″ x 5′6″
Warp: z2s brown & cream wool
Weft: Tan wool, 2 shots
Knot: Asymmetrical to the left

11. Balkan Isfahan 5′10″ x 9′5″
Warp: s8 cotton
Weft: Blue cotton, 2 shots
Knot: Asymmetrical to the left

12. Kurdish 4′5″ x 6′5″
Warp: z2s brown & dark brown wool
Weft: Brown wool, 1 shot
Knot: Symmetrical

13. Qashqai Kelim 5′8″ x 8′9″
Warp: z2s cream, brown, grey wool
Weft: Natural dyed wool, slit tapestry and
  supplementary weft

14. Bakhtiari 4′7″ x 6′8″
Warp: z7 cotton
Weft: Cotton, 2 shots
Knot: Symmetrical

15. Heriz 9′6″ x 14′11″
Warp: s15 cotton
Weft: White & light blue cotton, 2 shots
Knot: Symmetrical

16. Kurdish 7′11″ x 11′
Warp: z4 cotton
Weft: Tan & dark brown wool, 2 shots
Knot: Symmetrical

17. Caucasian
On right 2′6″ x 6′2″
Warp: z2s white and cream wool
Weft: Cotton, 2 shots
Knot: Symmetrical
On left 2′8″ x 6′1″
Warp: z2s ivory & tan wool
Weft: Cotton, 2 shots
Knot: Symmetrical

18. Baluche 1′7″ x 2′5″
Warp: z2s light tan wool
Weft: Dark brown wool, 2 shots
Knot: Asymmetrical to the right

19. Turkoman 6′10″ x 9′6″
Warp: z2s ivory wool
Weft: Light brown wool, 2 shots
Knot: Asymmetrical to the left

20. Kazak 4′2″ x 7′1″
Warp: z2s cream & light tan wool
Weft: Rose wool, 4 shots
Knot: Symmetrical

21. Bakhtiari 5′ x 6′9″
Warp: s2z cotton
Weft: Beige cotton, 1 shot
Knot: Symmetrical

22. Turkoman
Asmalyk 3′11″ x 1′6″
Warp: z2s brown & ivory wool
Weft: Brown & ivory wool, 2 shots
Knot: Symmetrical
Chuval 2′7″ x 3′9″
Warp: z2s light tan & ivory wool
Weft: Red wool, 2 shots
Knot: Asymmetrical to the left

Front cover:
Caucasian 4′1″ x 4′9″
Warp: z2s ivory & tan wool
Weft: Cotton, 2 shots
Knot: Symmetrical

Back cover:
Caucasian 3′3″ x 9′8″
Warp: z2s ivory wool
Weft: Cotton, 3-4 shots
Knot: Symmetrical

THE BREEMA RUG STUDY SOCIETY is composed of a group of people who see in the ancient art of oriental rug-weaving a unique aliveness and creativity. Members include professionals in the field as well as avid rug enthusiasts. They have established a research center to collect and document information on oriental rugs and frequently present lectures, workshops, exhibitions and tours. They are pleased to assist Mr. Winitz in the presentation of this book.

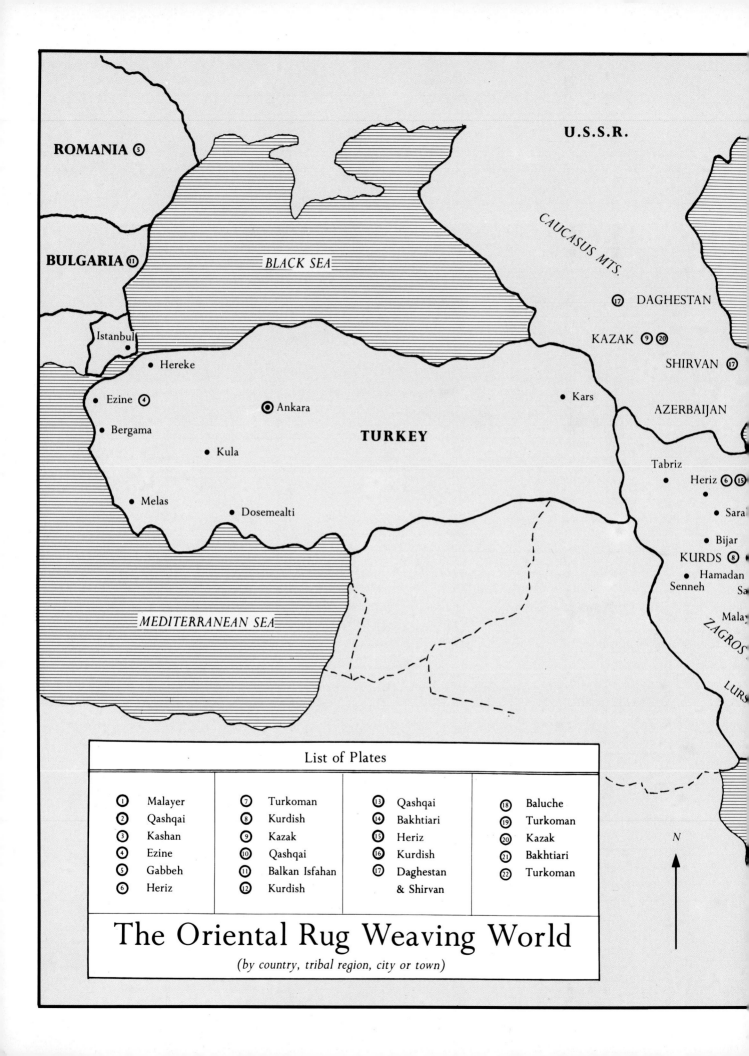

The Oriental Rug Weaving World
(by country, tribal region, city or town)